Science to the Rescue

Stranded on an Island

Can science save your life?

Gerry Bailey

Crabtree Publishing Company
www.crabtreebooks.com

Crabtree Publishing Company
www.crabtreebooks.com
1-800-387-7650

PMB 59051, 350 Fifth Ave.
59th Floor,
New York, NY 10118

616 Welland Ave.
St. Catharines, ON
L2M 5V6

Published by Crabtree Publishing in 2014

Author: Gerry Bailey
Illustrator: Leighton Noyes
Editor: Shirley Duke
Proofreader: Kathy Middleton
Production coordinator and
   Prepress technician: Tammy McGarr
Print coordinator: Margaret Amy Salter

Photographs:
All images are Shutterstock.com unless otherwise stated.
Cover - javarman, Yu Lan, Brian Lasenby, lightpoet,
lauraslens
Pg 1 - - Tatyana Vyc
Pg 2/3 - - nitrogenic.com   Pg 6 - mapichai
Pg 7 – (tl) lauraslens (tr) AridOcean (bl) Anton Balazh
(br) AridOcean Pg 8 - Neil Walton Photography
Pg 9 – (l) Designua (r) Konstantin Stepanenko
Pg 11 – Yu Lan Pg 12/13 - Muzhik
Pg 13 – (tl) Kuttelvaserova Stuchelova
(tr) Michael Zysman (b) Kidsana Maimeetook
Pg 15 – javarman   Pg 16 / 17 – javarman
Pg 17 – (tl) Bojan Bogdanovic
(tr) Steffen Foerster (m) Brendan van Son
(bl) foroyuinf (br) Images by Dr, Alan Lipkin
Pg 18 /19 - Mikhail_m_t
Pg 19 – (t) Vilainecrevette (m) Ethan Daniels
(b) Kristina Vackova
Pg 20 - (t) Maxim Tarasyugin (b) Pam Blizzard
Pg 23 – (t) Artur Tiutenko (b) angelo lano
Pg 24/25 – Neil Lang Pg 25 - Daniel j.Rao
Pg 26/27 – Thomas Barrat
Pg 29 – images.kew.org
Pg 30/31 - Tatyana Vyc
Both Frieze – zzveillust

Printed in Canada/082017/IH20170615

Library and Archives Canada Cataloguing in Publication

Bailey, Gerry, author
       Stranded on an island / Gerry Bailey.

(Science to the rescue)
Includes index.
Issued in print and electronic formats.
ISBN 978-0-7787-0430-0 (bound).--ISBN 978-0-7787-0436-2 (pbk.).--
ISBN 978-1-4271-7542-7 (html).--ISBN 978-1-4271-7548-9 (pdf)

      1. Islands--Juvenile literature. I. Title.

GB471.B35 2014   j551.42   C2014-900924-0
                                         C2014-900925-9

Library of Congress Cataloging-in-Publication Data

CIP available at Library of Congress

Contents

Joe's story

Hi! My name is Joe, and I've got a story to tell you—a real adventure!

I got stranded on a deserted island in the middle of the ocean. Although I knew someone would be by to pick me up at some point, I had to get by on my own until then.

I managed to survive with the help of all the science I knew and a great book I remembered reading about a guy named **Robinson Crusoe**.

But it's a long story. Let me tell you all about it...

How did I end up on an island all on my own?

I had set out from the **mainland** that morning and was rowing across to one of the islands not far from the shore. Everything was going well, until—CRACK! The boat hit a coral reef.

In moments, water was leaking in, and I needed to get myself to safety.

What is an island?

The **ocean floor** has all the same features we see on land—valleys, mountains, and volcanoes—but they lie in the ocean depths and are mostly hidden from view. However, sometimes the peaks of underwater mountains rise above the waves. They form small islands, either on their own or in groups.

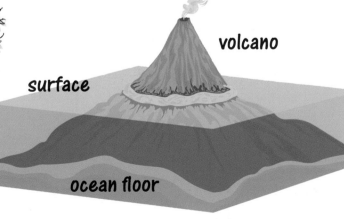

volcano

surface

ocean floor

Archipelagos

A group of islands is an **archipelago**. Indonesia is the largest archipelago in the world. It has 17,508 islands.

Islands are dotted throughout the world's oceans.

Greenland

The **Galapagos Islands** in the Pacific Ocean is an archipelago. The islands are named after the giant tortoises that live there.

Indonesia

The largest island in the world is Greenland, which lies near the North Pole. It's over 770,000 square miles (two million sq km) in size. Most islands are much smaller.

Galapagos Islands
San Salvador
Fernandina
Santa Cruz
Isabela
San Cristobal

Of course, I should have known! The coral often lies just under the surface of the waves and can't be seen. And it's jagged and sharp.

But here I was with a leaky boat, shipwrecked on an island in the middle of the ocean. I was just like Robinson Crusoe. Do you know that story?

Coral reefs

Coral is made up of the skeletons of living and dead sea creatures called polyps. They form reefs, or ridges, near islands in three ways: fringing (coral surrounds the base of an island), barrier (coral surrounds the island, but a bit farther away from it), and **atoll** (coral surrounds an underwater volcano and builds upward until a ring peeks above the water).

coral reef   lagoon

How do atolls grow?

A volcano erupts from the sea floor.

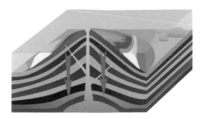

Coral grows on the underwater volcano.

Different kinds of plants begin to grow on the coral.

Island

An atoll coral reef encloses a ring of water called a **lagoon**.

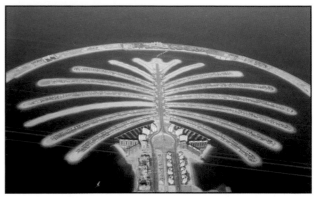

Dubai's Palm Jumeirah is a human-made island shaped like a plam tree.

Made by humans

Most islands are created naturally, but a few are made by humans. They are made to create extra land for homes, airports, or resorts.

Palm Jumeirah in the United Arab Emirates is an amazing human-made archipelago. The "tree" is joined to the mainland by a bridge. The island holds apartments and tourist resorts.

Luckily, *Robinson Crusoe* is a favorite story of mine. It was written about 300 years ago by Daniel Defoe, and it's about a sailor shipwrecked on a desert island.

Robinson Crusoe had to learn how to survive on his own. And he did—for 28 years!

He built a fenced-in home, hunted, grew barley and rice, and kept goats.

Crusoe was finally rescued by pirates. But by that time, he had found company.

One day he found footprints in the sand. He was not alone after all! Cannibals—people who eat people—had arrived on the island.

Crusoe bravely rescued a prisoner from the cannibals. Not knowing his language, Crusoe named him Friday because that was the day of his rescue.

The first thing Crusoe did was explore his new home, so I did the same. First I went in search of food.

People who live on islands call the coconut palm the "Tree of Life" because its fruit is so nutritious. It is rich in vitamins and minerals such as calcium, which helps bones grow. And there were coconuts everywhere!

Island plants

Once an island has a covering of soil, it can support plant life. Plants arrive as seeds, carried on the feathers or in the stomachs of birds. Other seeds are blown in by the wind or drift in on the ocean surface. They put down roots along the shore.

All parts of the coconut palm are useful. Besides the coconut fruit, the tree's leaves are used to make clothing, baskets, and medicines.

Seaweed

Bananas

The mangrove has long roots that dig down through the sand to fresher water.

Most plants cannot survive in salt water. The salt stops the flow of water through the plant's leaves. Some plants, like seaweed and **mangroves**, have skin-like barriers that stops salt from entering the roots. Others are able to get rid of salt using special parts, or glands, in their leaves.

Just like Crusoe, I needed to build a shelter. I thought it best to choose a spot where I could look out to sea and spot any boats or ships that might be passing.

I also needed to be close to fresh water.

So, just like Crusoe, I built my shelter using stakes as supports for the walls and drove these into the ground with a rock. I tied bamboo poles together with vines for the roof. Then I covered the whole structure with leafy branches and grass.

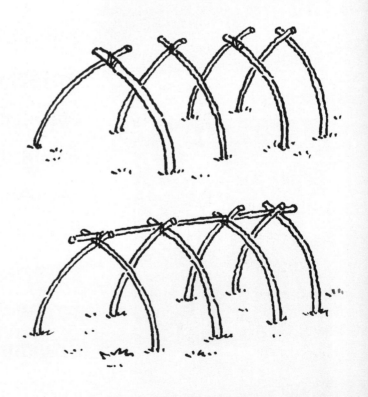

This home by the sea was built using cane poles as support and framing, and coconut leaves for the roof.

Island animals

Often the plants and animals found on islands have developed special features, or adaptations, as a result of having no contact with other animals, including humans. The giant tortoise of the Galapagos Islands is a good example.

Giant tortoises used to live in all parts of the world. Over time they changed and became smaller by sharing and mixing **genes**. Because the Galapagos Islands are isolated, tortoises there did not mix their genes and had fewer **predators**. Today, they are one of only two groups of giant tortoises left in the world. These land-dwellers can live for over 100 years.

After studying the animals of the Galapagos, **naturalist** Charles Darwin, took home over 50 giant tortoises. The crew of his ship ate them and tossed the shells.

The marine iguana lives on land and feeds on algae in **tide pools** and underwater.

The blue-footed booby lives on land but dives from great heights to catch anchovies, sardines, or flying fish.

Smaller turtles that live in the sea must scurry from where they hatch on the beach to reach the safety of the water. Most are eaten by predators first.

A male frigate bird tries to attract a mate by puffing up his red throat sac.

Life in the coral reef

The coral polyps that make
up a coral reef are tiny,
tube-shaped animals. Each
polyp grows a skeleton made
of the same material that is in
limestone, a hard, durable rock
used in building construction.
The coral skeletons form fantastic
shapes under water: curly leaves, lacy fans, or tiny pipes.

Tropical fish swim along the reef, searching for food. They include neon-colored angelfish, striped, spiny lionfish, and tiny sea horses. Other animals that live in the reef include sea stars, sponges, and worms. They eat plants such as algae and sea grasses.

Butterflyfish swim with other coral reef fish.

The blue sea star waves an arm to catch passing food.

The male sea horse is the one that cares for the eggs.

How to catch fish

Once nearly extinct, brown pelicans are skilled at catching fish. They have huge beaks, or bills, that are over three feet long (0.9 m). The bill has a large pouch. Their six-foot (2 m) wingspan helps them glide easily.

They plunge into the sea and scoop out as much as two gallons (9 L) of water in their pouches. The water drains out through the sides of the bill and fish trapped inside are quickly eaten.

Learning how to fish in this way is difficult, and young birds that don't learn the skill do not survive.

I watched the pelicans for some time. That's clever, I thought. But I can't dive in after the fish, and I can't swallow all that water.

However, I could make a spear. I used the lining of my pocket to tie my knife to a pole.

I found a rock near the shallow water and stood waiting for my chance. With my spear raised, I watched silently until a shadow moved in the water, then I struck!

I had caught my first fish.

I needed to cook the fish, which meant I had to light a fire.

Robinson Crusoe probably had a flint in his **musket**. Flint is a hard stone that can be used to make sparks. But I had nothing like that!

1. To make a fire plow, you need two pieces of wood. Place some dry grass, called tinder, under the upright stick.

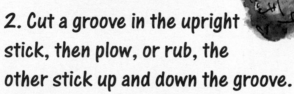

2. Cut a groove in the upright stick, then plow, or rub, the other stick up and down the groove.

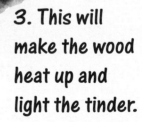

3. This will make the wood heat up and light the tinder.

I had lit my fire the hard way—using heat made by **friction**.

Friction

When two objects are rubbed together, an energy called friction is created. Friction is a force that slows down things that are moving. Less friction is created between smooth surfaces than rough ones.

However, all friction results in heat. If two surfaces rub against each other, they start to heat up. One way to create enough heat to set fire to a dry twig or piece of grass is to rub a pointed stick into a hole made in another piece of wood.

The Maasai people of Kenya are a semi-nomadic people, which means they move from place to place as they herd their cattle and goats. They rely on traditional ways such as using friction to make fire.

Cooking food makes it easier to eat and digest.

Perhaps it was the tempting smell of the fish, but the next morning, just like Crusoe, I knew I'd had a visitor in the night.

Footprints led away from my home, across the sand, and into the distance. Human footprints!

I was not alone on the island after all!

I peered up and down the beach. Nobody! But I had an odd feeling I was being watched.

And I was! I turned to see a man casting his net in the shallow water. He was trapping fish in the net and gently pulling it to shore. When he saw me, he folded the net, waved, and called me over.

Had I found my own friend, Friday?

To fish with a net, the fisher gathers ten handfuls of net in one hand and one in the other. Both hands release at the same time the net is thrown.

His name was Tonwhu. He told me he visited the island often to fish. I was lucky, because now he would take me back to the mainland in his fishing boat, where I could rejoin my team.

But first, he wanted to show me something that had been made 3,000 years ago. That was when his ancestors, or his family of long ago, had first arrived on the isand.

Island peoples

The islands of the Pacific Ocean known as Polynesia and Melanesia were first settled by seafaring people from Asia. They made their amazing voyage of nearly 2,500 miles (3,218 km) to the islands in great canoes.

1,000 stone Moai guard the islands.

Easter Island was one of the most distant islands to be inhabited. The island soon developed its own culture, including the only written language in the region. Rock and wood carvings still remain that show the people playing music and dancing.

Massive stone carvings called Moai represent the spirits of their ancient Polynesian ancestors. Most face away from the ocean toward the villages to guard over the people. They were likely carved in a quarry and transported to the coast by walking them or using a sled or rollers.

Tonwhu promised to take me back to the mainland in his fishing boat. However, he also said he would help me explore the island before we left.

He knew where there were some rare plants, and he would help me gather some seeds so I could take them back with me.

Rare plants

Things living on an island that are not found anywhere else are known as the island's native plants and animals.

All the plants and animals that are native to the Galapagos Islands, for example, originally came from somewhere else. But they arrived very slowly. In the 3 million years that the islands have existed, one new species has arrived every 10,000 years.

Native island plants are precious because they are found nowhere else.

Why is Joe there?

Scientists like Joe visit the islands to study native seeds and try to find out how the first plants looked and were spread. They also gather samples of the seeds they find.

People need plants. They give us oxygen to breathe, food, clothing, and even medicine. Scientists are setting up seed banks to protect plants from disappearing from Earth.

Seed banks contain seeds that have been frozen so they can be saved a long time in case certain crops are ever destroyed or die out. Frozen wheat, barley, and pea seeds can last up to 1,000 years.

Seeds are kept in powerful cooling units, frozen at 0°F (-18°C).

There are about 1,400 seed banks around the world. The most famous is the **Svalbard Global Seed Vault** in Norway, which holds seeds of 700,000 plants.

Glossary

archipelago
A group of islands separated from the mainland, that sometimes forms a chain

atoll
A circular coral reef that attaches beneath the rim of an underwater volcano and builds up over time until it grows above the surface

friction
A force created by two surfaces rubbing together, resulting in heat and loss of motion

Galapagos Islands
An archipelago of 18 major islands lying off the west coast of South America. The islands are famous for their wildlife.

genes
Chemical information about biological traits, or features, that is passed from parent to child

lagoon
A shallow lake of salt water that is often cut off from the sea by a ridge of coral

limestone
A kind of rock that has formed over millions of years as dirt, mud, and other rock particles have settled and pressed into layers

mainland
A body of land that is part of a continent; not detached or offshore

mangrove
A plants with lots of deep roots that can grow in salt water

musket
A firearm used by soldiers long ago

naturalist
A person who studies plants and animals

ocean floor
The surface of the land under the ocean which has valleys and mountains like the land above

predators
Animals that hunt other animals for food

Robinson Crusoe
The hero of author Daniel Defoe's story about a castaway on an island

Svalbard Global Seed Vault
The largest and most important collection of seeds in the world located inside a mountain on an island halfway between Norway and the North Pole

tide pools
A pool of salt water and animals left among rocks when the tide goes out

Learn More...

Books:

Survive on a Desert Island (Survival Challenge)
by Claire Llewellyn.
Silver Dolphin Books, 2006

The Complete Book of Fire: Building Campfires for Warmth, Light, Cooking, and Survival
by Buck Tilton.
Menasha Ridge Press, 2005

Coral Reefs (Eye to Eye with Endangered Habitats)
by Precious McKenzie.
Rourke Publishing, 2011

Websites:

Learn survival skills on a deserted island:
http://traveltips.usatoday.com/survival-guide-deserted-island-62359.html

Find out how to build a campfire:
www.instructables.com/id/How-to-Build-a-Fire-without-a-match-or-a-lighter/

Get the facts on Svalbard Global Seed Vault, the world's largest seed bank:
www.croptrust.org/content/svalbard-global-seed-vault

Index